STUD

FATHOM BIBLE STUDIES

FATH●M

A DEEP DIVE INTO THE STORY OF GOD

the birth of the kingdom
FROM SAUL TO SOLOMON

FATHOM: THE BIRTH OF THE KINGDOM
FROM SAUL TO SOLOMON
STUDENT JOURNAL

Scripture quotations are taken from the Common English Bible, copyright 2011. Used by permission. All rights reserved.

Writer: Lyndsey Medford
Editor: Ben Howard
Designer: Keely Moore

Websites are constantly changing. Although the websites recommended in this resource were checked at the time this unit was developed, we recommend that you double-check all sites to verify that they are still live and that they are still suitable for students before doing the activity.

ISBN: 9781501841583
PACP10513503-01

18 19 20 21 22 23 24 25 26 27 — 10 9 8 7 6 5 4 3 2 1

MANUFACTURED IN THE UNITED STATES OF AMERICA

CONTENTS

About Fathom

Fathom.

It's such a big word. It feels endless and deep. It's the kind of word that feels like it should only be uttered by James Earl Jones with the bass turned all the way up.

Which means it's the perfect word to talk about a God who's infinite and awe-inspiring. It's also the perfect word for a book like the Bible that's filled with miracles and inspiration, but also wrestles with stories of violence and pain and loss.

The mission of *Fathom* is to dive deep into the story of God that we find in the Bible. You'll encounter Scriptures filled with inspiration and encouragement, and you'll also explore passages that are more complicated and challenging.

Each lesson will focus on one passage, but will also launch into the larger context of how God's story is being told through that passage. More importantly, each lesson will explore how God's story is intimately tied to our own stories, and how a God who is beyond our imagination can also be a God who loves us deeply and personally.

We invite you to wrestle with this and more as we dive deep into God's story.

Welcome

This book is yours. Or at least, it will be.

This book is designed to assist you as you explore, engage, and wrestle with everything that you'll experience over the next four weeks.

Each week during this study, this book will be filled with Scripture, activities, and questions to encourage and inspire you while you work your way through the Bible with your friends.

While we'll offer suggestions on how to use this journal, we want you to truly make it yours. Fill it with ideas and prayers. Take notes. Draw. Write poetry. Express yourself! Do whatever it is you need to do to help you remember what you've learned here.

Let this book be your canvas for creativity and self-expression. Let it be a place for honest questions and emotions that you may not feel comfortable expressing anywhere else, because at the end of this study, this book is yours.

You can use it to remember and reflect on what you learned, or you can use it to keep studying on your own, to keep questioning and exploring. We've included two sections at the end, "Takeaway" and "Explore More," to help you in that quest.

As you begin, we pray that you encounter the majesty and love of God through this study. We pray that you dive deep into the story of God and creation, and we pray that you find peace and hope in these lessons.

The Fathom 66   <small>Bible Genre Guide</small>

ENTER ZIP OR LOCATION [　　　　　]

Stories ♡   [TICKETS]
★★★★★
Showtimes: Parts of Genesis, Joshua, Judges, Ruth, 1 Samuel,
2 Samuel, 1 Kings, 2 Kings, 1 Chronicles, 2 Chronicles, Ezra,
Nehemiah, Esther, Matthew, Mark, Luke, John, Acts

The Law ♡   [TICKETS]
★★★★★
Showtimes: Parts of Genesis, Exodus, Leviticus, Numbers,
Deuteronomy

Wisdom ♡   [TICKETS]
★★★★★
Showtimes: Job, Some Psalms, Proverbs, Ecclesiastes,
Song of Solomon, Lamentations, James

Psalms ♡   [TICKETS]
★★★★★
Showtimes: Psalms

The Prophets ♡   [TICKETS]
★★★★★
Showtimes: Isaiah, Jeremiah, Ezekiel, Hosea, Joel, Amos, Obadiah,
Jonah, Michah, Nahum, Habakkuk, Zephaniah, Haggai, Zechariah,
Malachi

Letters ♡   [TICKETS]
★★★★★
Showtimes: Romans, 1 Corinthians, 2 Corinthians, Galatians, Ephesians,
Philippians, Colossians, 1 Thessalonians, 2 Thessalonians, 1 Timothy, 2 Timothy,
Titus, Philemon, Hebrews, James, 1 Peter, 2 Peter, 1 John, 2 John, 3 John, Jude

Apocalyptic Writings ♡   [TICKETS]
★★★★★
Showtimes: Daniel, Revelation

The Fathom Bible Storylines

Create   1

Invite   I

Act   A

Redeem   R

Experience   E

Hope   H

Introduction to The Birth of the Kingdom

Background

Like a Shakesperean play, the complicated saga about the birth of the kingdom of Israel can be a daunting read. It is filled with extremely complex characters, unfamiliar role players, and a number of other confusing cultural artifacts. Like one of Shakespeare's plays, these stories serve as both history and a meditation on the human condition. Even though the action is propelled by political schemes, international intrigue, and violent wars that may make it feel far removed from our own lives, the fears, joys, and struggles of the main characters are intimately familiar.

There is Samuel, the weary—and often crabby—prophet assigned to corral both the people and the new king to keep God first amidst the nation's transition. We can feel his irritation and disappointment, but also his hope that God will guide and sustain Israel to do what it has been commanded. We sympathize, too, with Saul, the reluctant king turned insecure leader. Who, when pushed to the point of desperation, hasn't tried to take matters into their own hands? Who hasn't made things worse in the process? We watch Saul make these mistakes over and over, hoping that he will learn from them and live up to his early promise. But instead, his destruction becomes ever more assured.

David fascinates us. He is emotional, but he is strong. He is cunning and a natural leader, but ill-suited to life in a palace. His mistakes and shortcomings are no less deplorable than Saul's, but the pattern that repeats in David's life is one of childlike faith, not fear and pride. From David's story, we learn that superhuman holiness and great ability are not what is required of us, but humility and reliance on God. Solomon also demonstrates these virtues, and we can connect with his earnest desire to do the right thing. But, like his father, Solomon also has his demons and is forced to battle with the temptations of power and comfort.

While we can't delve into every nook and cranny of these stories and these characters in four weeks, we can keep the broader story in mind as we journey along. This study offers several ways to engage with the characters listed previously at different points throughout their lives. As you encounter episodes that intrigue you, take note of them and read further on your own. Through the stories of Samuel, Saul, David, and Solomon, we recognize ourselves. We see how God guides, teaches, convicts, forgives, and loves us in the midst of our victories and in our follies. God is with us, no matter what.

Fathom Strategy for Reading and Understanding the Bible

"The Bible is written for us, but not to us."

This is where we start on our quest. When we read the Bible, we have to constantly remember that the Bible is written for us, but not to us. Understanding the original context of the Bible helps us ask the right questions when interpreting Scripture.

For the first steps in our process, we need to understand how each passage we read functions in context and examine the historical background. When we read a passage, we should ask questions about the era, location, and culture of the original audience, as well as how a particular writing relates to the larger narrative of the Bible. This strategy not only helps us understand a passage's primary meaning, it also gives us guidance on how to translate that meaning into our specific circumstances today.

Saul Loses His Kingdom

Summary

This week you'll learn about Saul's development over the course of his reign and the events that lead him to lose God's favor. You'll also learn about the importance of following God's instructions and being obedient to God.

Overview

- **Sync** with the themes of 1 and 2 Samuel through a group game.
- **Tour** through the story of Saul's disobedience by reading and acting out the narrative.
- **Reveal** more about the meaning of Saul's disobedience by discussing it in small groups.
- **Build** on the themes of 1 and 2 Samuel by writing an epic poem about Saul's life.
- **After** the lesson, choose an activity to help you reflect on obedience throughout the week.

Anchor Point

- 1 Samuel 15:22—*Does the Lord want entirely burned offerings and sacrifices as much as obedience to the Lord? Listen to this: obeying is better than sacrificing, paying attention is better than fat from rams.*

Blindfolded Maze

Instructions

1. Pick a partner.
2. Choose one partner to be the builder/guide and the other to be the walker.
3. The builder/guide will go into a separate room to build a maze with the other builders/guides.
4. Once complete, each team will attempt to navigate the maze with the walker blindfolded.
5. The builder/guide can only direct the walker using their voice.
6. Multiple teams will likely be in the maze at the same time.

• How did it feel to be blindfolded on an unfamiliar path? How did it feel to give instructions to a blindfolded person?

Whenever we're trying to decide what to do, we can feel like we are blindfolded with unknown obstacles in front of us. In today's story, Saul responds to this feeling of vulnerability by taking matters into his own hands, but this leads him into a trap.

Word Association

Rules

1. The leader will say a word; for example, "Tree."
2. The leader will then point at someone.
3. That person will respond with the first thing that comes to mind; for example, "Bark."
4. They will then point to someone, and the cycle will repeat until the leader introduces a new word.

• Based on our associations, what are some things our group thinks about kings and kingship?

Today we're beginning our look at the stories of 1 and 2 Samuel. All the words that started new rounds represent something from these books that focus on the beginnings of Israel's kingdom and the men who took on the role of king.

NARRATOR #1: Though Saul was tall, good-looking, and hardworking, no one ever expected him to be king. He was simply a young man who worked for his father, like all the other young men. However, when the people clamored for a king, asking the revered prophet Samuel to anoint a military leader to protect them from their neighbors, Samuel saw king material in Saul. At first, Saul literally hid from his new calling, but the people backed him anyway, especially when he won his first military victory.

- *Does this sound like any heroes you know of? What do you think it says about Saul that he was reluctant to be king?*

NARRATOR #2: Battle by battle, Saul settled into the role. The people were getting what they wanted as Saul and his son led them to victory over their enemies. Saul was losing his former timidity, but we have to wonder if he ever lost his feelings of inadequacy. Not long after the beginning of his rule, Saul began to make rash decisions and would have emotional outbursts out of fear: fear of the future and fear of imaginary enemies. He never seemed to trust that things might go well for him—and it caused him to sabotage himself.

- *Do you think Saul's personality changed when he became king? If so, how do you think it shifted?*

NARRATOR #1: Once, Saul was waiting for Samuel to make sacrifices to God on Saul's behalf before a battle. Finally, Saul and his men became too anxious to wait any longer, and Saul offered the sacrifices himself, though he'd been instructed to wait for Samuel. When Samuel arrived, he told Saul he'd been foolish, but Saul did not take this chance to learn from his mistakes.

NARRATOR #2: On another occasion, Saul swore to kill any man who ate food before a battle was won. However, Saul's son, Jonathan, hadn't heard about the oath, and when he found some honey, he ate it. Only the outrage of the other soldiers saved Jonathan from his father that day.

- *What do these two stories tell us about Saul's character?*

NARRATOR #1: Finally, Samuel gave Saul a message from God, that he should go in battle against the Amalekites and kill every living thing as a sacrifice to God. Saul went and destroyed the enemy, but he left some things alive.

This may sound like a merciful act, but it wasn't. Saul did not spare the women and children. Instead, Saul spared the best of the cattle, which he brought back to feast on, and the king, who he paraded through the streets to gloat about his victory.

- *These stories take place over years and years. How have we seen Saul change over the course of his reign?*

The following is adapted from Samuel 15:13-34.

NARRATOR #2: Samuel went looking for Saul, and was told that Saul had made a monument in his own honor before going on to the feast he'd planned. Eventually, Samuel found him, and Saul greeted him with a huge grin.

"Hello, friend! I've done what God told us!"

But Samuel asked, "Then what are all these cattle doing here?"

Saul now realized that his victory in battle had not been a free pass to do whatever he wanted. He innocently replied, "We brought them back to sacrifice to the LORD!"

"Stop!" Samuel cried. "I have brought a message from God!

"Although you were once small in your own eyes, did you not become the head of the tribes of Israel? The LORD anointed you king. And he sent you on a mission. Why did you not obey the LORD? Why did you pounce on the plunder and do evil?"

"But I did obey the LORD," Saul whined. "I destroyed the Amalekites and brought back their king. The soldiers took the cattle to sacrifice them."

NARRATOR #1: Saul replied, "Does the LORD want entirely burned offerings and sacrifices as much as obedience to the LORD? Listen to this: obeying is better than sacrificing, paying attention is better than fat from rams, because rebellion is as bad as the sin of divination; arrogance is like the evil of idolatry. Because you have rejected what the LORD said, he has rejected you as king."

Saul begged for another chance, but he'd already been given several. Samuel had nothing left to say to him. "Bring me Agag the king of the Amalekites!" he roared, and Samuel killed Agag.

NARRATOR #2: Saul would still be king for a long time, but he knew that his son would never succeed him. What he didn't know was that David was already being anointed as the next king. Saul's military career was over, and many more chapters of 1 Samuel chronicle his conflict with David, his slow descent into madness, and his eventual suicide in battle.

• *In five words, how would you describe King Saul? What does King Saul's story teach us about following God?*

1) _____

2) _____

3) _____

4) _____

5) _____

Take a few minutes to silently journal about the prompt you've been assigned. Once finished, discuss your responses with your group.

Journal Questions

Group 1

• Why do you think Saul disobeyed the entire order to destroy the Amalekites? Why doesn't Samuel accept his reasoning?

Group 2

• Do you think God gives us specific instructions today, like God gave to Saul? How do we know when we are obeying incompletely, or with mixed motives?

Group 3

• How do you understand the violence in this story? Is it God's prerogative to order people to murder? Has something about God or religion changed since this story took place?

BUILD FATH●M

Important Moments from the Life of King Saul

- Saul is born in the tenth century BCE (Before Common Era).
- As a young man, Samuel anoints Saul to be the first king of Israel.
- Soon afterward, Saul wins a battle for a besieged Israelite city.
- Saul fails to wait for Samuel to perform a sacrifice before a battle and, instead does it himself. Samuel rebukes him for his lack of trust.
- Saul eventually wins the battle.
- Before the next battle, Saul threatens to kill anyone in the army who eats before they win. His son doesn't hear about it and eats some honey he finds. The men in the army have to rescue Saul's son from being killed.
- Saul fails to kill King Agag (today's story).
- David kills Goliath and the people begin to sing his praises, making Saul jealous.
- Saul requires David to live at the palace.
- David becomes a successful military officer.
- Eventually, Saul swears to kill David, and David flees.
- Saul repeatedly gathers search parties to find and kill David.
- David has multiple opportunities to sneak up on Saul and kill him instead, but spares his life out of respect for the monarchy.
- Years after first swearing to kill David, Saul goes into battle against the Philistines. Three of his sons die, and he is wounded. He commits suicide in the midst of the battle rather than be killed by an enemy.

BUILD   FATH◉M

Work with your group to create an epic poem of at least fifteen lines. Use the space provided below to work on your poem.

_____

_____

_____

_____

_____

_____

_____

_____

_____

_____

_____

_____

_____

_____

(15)
_____

_____

_____

_____

AFTER

Tales of Obedience

Read through another story in the Bible that talks about obedience. *(Tip: Exodus 19, Nehemiah 13, and John 17 all do.)* Write a verse from this story that reminds you of its central message, and post it somewhere you will see it in the morning. Spend five minutes reflecting on what that verse means to you this week.

What story do you want focus on this week?

_____

Write out a verse from this story that reminds you of its central message.

_____

_____

_____

Confess Disobedience

Saul was disobedient, and it ended up costing him his kingdom and his relationship with God. This week tell a friend about a time when you were disobedient and what it cost you. Ask them to share a similar situation.

Who is someone you can share with this week?

_____

Three Kings

Over the next few weeks, we will be studying Saul, David, and Solomon, the first three kings of Israel. This week ask your family members and friends what they know about these three kings. Share with them something that you learned from our lesson today.

Who are three family members or friends you can ask about Saul, David, and Solomon this week?

1) _____

2) _____

3) _____

What is one thing you learned from this lesson that you can share with them?

_____

PRARER

God, thank you that your commands are given for our own good, even when we can't clearly see how that is. Holy Spirit, convict us and empower us to obey you with faith and joy. Amen.

David Dancing

Summary

You will learn about David's character through the story of how he rejoiced before the Lord. You will also learn to celebrate God, no matter who is watching.

Overview

- **Sync** with the experience of being undignified by dancing together.
- **Tour** through David's dancing day with immersive storytelling.
- **Reveal** the emotions of the story by journaling about your own stories.
- **Build** on these thoughts by talking about other ways David didn't fit into his roles.
- **After** the lesson, take the risk of being undignified!

Anchor Point

- 2 Samuel 6:21—*I was celebrating before the Lord, who chose me over your father and his entire family, and who appointed me leader over the Lord's people, over Israel—and I will celebrate before the Lord again!*

Make Someone Else Dance Like Nobody's Watching

Instructions

1) Split into groups of four.
2) Split your group of four into two pairs.
3) With your partner, make up a dance routine.
4) Teach your dance to the other pair in your group.
5) Perform the dance made for you for everyone.
6) The pair that makes up the silliest dance will win a prize.

• What would it take for you to do that dance in front of your school or somewhere bigger, like the halftime show of a football game?

Today we're learning about a day when David was so happy that he made a fool of himself and danced in front of an entire city. He cared more about celebrating God than about preserving his dignity as the king.

Highs and Lows

Instructions

1) On the first index card you were given, write down a two- or three-sentence description of one of the happiest moments in your life.
2) On the other index card, write down a two- or three-sentence description of one of the most embarrassing moments in your life.
3) Fold them in half and place them in the bowl at the front of the room.
4) The leader will read out each card one at a time, and you will guess who wrote each one.
5) Give yourself a point for each answer you get correct.

Your Points:

Some people might say that King David's best moment and most embarrassing moment occurred at the same time. As we hear today's story, try to remember your own thoughts and feelings during the moments you described.

TOUR

FATH●M

Read the passage you've been assigned, and think about how you would have experienced this story through the eyes of David. Keep in mind the short synopsis of David's story that you've heard so far.

2 Samuel 6:1-11

Once again David assembled the select warriors of Israel, thirty thousand strong. David and all the troops who were with him set out for Baalah, which is Kiriath-jearim of Judah, to bring God's chest up from there—the chest that is called by the name of the Lord of heavenly forces, who sits enthroned on the winged creatures. They loaded God's chest on a new cart and carried it from Abinadab's house, which was on the hill. Uzzah and Ahio, Abinadab's sons, were driving the new cart. Uzzah was beside God's chest while Ahio was walking in front of it. Meanwhile, David and the entire house of Israel celebrated in the Lord's presence with all their strength, with songs, zithers, harps, tambourines, rattles, and cymbals.

When they approached Nacon's threshing floor, Uzzah reached out to God's chest and grabbed it because the oxen had stumbled. The Lord became angry at Uzzah, and God struck him there because of his mistake, and he died there next to God's chest. Then David got angry because the Lord's anger lashed out against Uzzah, and so that place is called Perez-uzzah today.

David was frightened by the Lord that day. "How will I ever bring the Lord's chest to me?" he asked. So David didn't take the chest away with him to David's City. Instead, he had it put in the house of Obed-edom, who was from Gath. The Lord's chest stayed with Obed-edom's household in Gath for three months, and the Lord blessed Obed-edom's household and all that he had.

TOUR

In your group, come up with a way to share your half of the story with the rest of the class in two to three minutes. Use the space provided below for notes.

_____

_____

_____

_____

_____

_____

_____

_____

_____

_____

_____

2 Samuel 6:12-23

King David was told, "The Lord has blessed Obed-edom's family and everything he has because of God's chest being there." So David went and brought God's chest up from Obed-edom's house to David's City with celebration. Whenever those bearing the chest advanced six steps, David sacrificed an ox and a fatling calf. David, dressed in a linen priestly vest, danced with all his strength before the Lord. This is how David and the entire house of Israel brought up the Lord's chest with shouts and trumpet blasts.

As the Lord's chest entered David's City, Saul's daughter Michal was watching from a window. She saw King David jumping and dancing before the Lord, and she lost all respect for him.

The Lord's chest was brought in and put in its place inside the tent that David had pitched for it. Then David offered entirely burned offerings in the Lord's presence in addition to well-being sacrifices. When David finished offering the entirely burned offerings and the well-being sacrifices, he blessed the people in the name of the Lord of heavenly forces. He distributed food among all the people of Israel—to the whole crowd, male and female—each receiving a loaf of bread, a date cake, and a raisin cake. Then all the people went back to their homes.

David went home to bless his household, but Saul's daughter Michal came out to meet him. "How did Israel's king honor himself today?" she said. "By exposing himself in plain view of the female servants of his subjects like any indecent person would!"

David replied to Michal, "I was celebrating before the Lord, who chose me over your father and his entire family, and who appointed me leader over the Lord's people, over Israel—and I will celebrate before the Lord again! I may humiliate myself even more, and I may be humbled in my own eyes, but I will be honored by the female servants you are talking about!"

Michal, Saul's daughter, had no children to the day she died.

TOUR

FATH●M

In your group, come up with a way to share your half of the story with the rest of the class in two to three minutes. Use the space provided below for notes.

_____

_____

_____

_____

_____

_____

_____

_____

_____

_____

_____

REVEAL FATH●M

Spend the next few minutes responding to the questions below. When you're done journaling, turn to a friend and share either one of the moments you described or a thought that came to you while responding to these questions.

Journal Questions

• When and where have you been happy enough to dance? Put yourself back in that moment and describe it. What did you see, hear, smell, and feel? What led up to that moment? What did you do? Why were you so happy?

• When and where do you feel that you are most yourself? What makes you feel firmly rooted or held by God? Respond to this question as if you are speaking directly to God.

BUILD

What words or phrases would you use to describe the following three people?

• Man

• King

• Holy Person

Descriptions of David

- David played the harp. (1 Samuel 16:18)
- David was uncomfortable wearing armor. (1 Samuel 17:39)
- David and Jonathan, Saul's son, were inseparable; they loved each other. (1 Samuel 18:3)
- After fleeing from Saul, David led a band of distressed, indebted, and discontented men who wanted to resist Saul. (1 Samuel 22:2)
- David had the chance to kill Saul, but let him go out of respect for the monarchy God had established. (1 Samuel 24:6)
- David lived among Israel's enemies, the Philistines, and fought on their behalf. (1 Samuel 28:1)
- David kept his oaths. (1 Samuel 30:15, 23)
- David often prayed and asked God questions to help him decide what to do. (2 Samuel 2:1; 7:18)

What's one way you identify with David, either from the list above or from another story you know?

Can't Hold It In

Think of a time when you were so happy that you just wanted to dance and worship God. Make a piece of art or write a short paragraph expressing your joy and share it on social media.

When have you been so happy that you just wanted to dance?

_____

How could you express that joy on social media?

_____

_____

Playing a Role

Michal was upset at David because she didn't think he was acting in the way that was expected of him, but David knew that worship was more important than playing a role. Is there some way in which you feel you don't fit into a role you're expected to play? Share with a friend and talk about how you might navigate that tension.

Who can you talk to about this question this week?

_____

Be Like David

Choose one of the characteristics from the Build activity that stands out to you about David. This week read the chapter cited for that characteristic. Keep that trait in mind this week, and pray to God to show you what it might mean to put this trait into practice in your own life.

Which characteristic of David stands out to you?

_____

What chapter is associated with that characteristic?

_____

PRAYER

As a class, try out this short dance-prayer.

(Spreading your arms out wide.)

Thank you, God, for our . . .

(Wave your arms in a fluid motion.)

. . . creativity and our . . .

(Bring your fists into your heart.)

. . . emotions.

(Hug yourself.)

Let us embrace . . .

(Wave some jazz hands and spin around in a circle.)

. . . becoming undignified for you. Amen.

Nathan Calls David to Justice

Summary

In this lesson, you will explore the story Nathan tells to help David see his sin in ordering Uriah's death. This lesson will focus on David's abuse of power and the importance of seeking out wise counsel from people who will tell us hard truths.

Overview

- **Sync** with the theme of how power can be abused by playing a game.
- **Tour** through the story of David and Bathsheba in a staged reading.
- **Reveal** the themes present in this story through journaling and group discussion.
- **Build** on the themes of the story by retelling and illustrating the story.
- **After** the lesson, find ways to engage deeply in relationships that make us better.

Anchor Point

- Proverbs 19:20-21—*Listen to advice and accept instruction, so you might grow wise in the future. Many plans are in a person's mind, but the LORD's purpose will succeed.*

Silver Spoon

Rules

1) Everyone needs to back their chair away from the table so that they can barely reach the table with their arms extended.
2) You must stay seated in your chair at all times.
3) Everyone will receive four cards to start.
4) The rest of the cards go to the dealer.
5) Your goal is to collect four of a kind (for example, 4 aces or 4 nines).
6) You must always have four cards in your hand.
7) The dealer will begin by looking at the top card. They will choose to pass it, or keep it and pass one of their other cards.
8) The cards will then be passed around the table, and each player will have the same option.
9) When someone has four of a kind, they will grab a spoon.
10) When you see someone else grab a spoon, you should take one too.
11) The person left without a spoon will be out.

• How did you feel when the serving spoon was placed in front of one person? Do you think that person had an advantage?

In today's story, King David abuses his advantages and powers as king to get what he wants. Today we're going to learn about God's response to how God views the role of justice.

King's Odds

Rules

1) Split into three equal groups.
2) This game will follow the same basic rules as "War."
3) Everyone will put down a card. The person with the highest card wins the hand and keeps all the cards played.
4) If two people tie, they will face off again, and the person with the highest cards will get all the cards from both rounds.
5) The goal is to get all the cards in the deck.
6) Whoever wins the first hand will be named the king.
7) Anytime the king loses a hand, they are allowed an extra chance and can turn over the next card. If the new card is the highest, they win and keep all the cards.
8) Everyone else must play normally.

• How many of the kings won? What would have been different if the king had the same odds as everyone else?

In today's story, King David abuses his power as king to get what he wants. Today we're going to learn about God's response to how God views the role of justice.

The following script is adapted from 2 Samuel 11–12.

STORYTELLER #1: In the spring, when kings go off to war, King David stayed home and sent some other people off to war.

STORYTELLER #2: One day he woke up from his afternoon nap and went out on the rooftop of the palace. From there, he saw a beautiful woman bathing and told his servants to find out who she was.

STORYTELLER #1: Which is pretty creepy when you think about it.

STORYTELLER #2: They told him her name was Bathsheba, and she was the wife of one of his soldiers—you know, the ones who were out fighting on his behalf. David sent his messengers to get her and when she came to him, he had sex with her.

STORYTELLER #1: A few weeks later, Bathsheba sent David a message that she was pregnant.

STORYTELLER #2: David devised a plan. He called Bathsheba's husband, Uriah, back from the battlefield as if to ask him how things were going. Then he told Uriah to go home and enjoy himself.

STORYTELLER #1: But Uriah never went into his house, let alone enjoyed his wife's charms. Even when David got him drunk, he slept outside the palace in solidarity with his soldiers still out fighting.

STORYTELLER #2: So David sent a message back with Uriah to Uriah's commander. "Put Uriah on the front lines of the fighting," he said.

STORYTELLER #1: The commander not only put Uriah on the front lines, but sent the army closer to the enemy than necessary. Many men died, including Uriah.

STORYTELLER #2: After a couple of weeks, David sent for Bathsheba again and married her. What David had done was evil in the eyes of the Lord.

STORYTELLER #1: David's friend, the prophet Nathan, came to visit David. He shared the following story.

NATHAN: There were two men in the same city—one rich, one poor. The rich man had a lot of sheep and cattle, but the poor man had nothing—just one small ewe lamb that he had bought. He raised that lamb, and it grew up with him and his children. It would eat from his food and drink from his cup—even sleep in his arms! It was like a daughter to him.

NATHAN: Now a traveler came to visit the rich man, but the rich man wasn't willing to take anything from his own flock or herd to prepare for the guest who had arrived. Instead, he took the poor man's ewe lamb and prepared it for the visitor.

STORYTELLER #1: David got very angry at the man, and he said to Nathan, "The one who did this is demonic! He must restore the ewe lamb seven times over because he did this and because he had no compassion." To which Nathan replied . . .

NATHAN: You are that man! This is what the LORD God of Israel says: I anointed you king over Israel and delivered you from Saul's power. I gave your master's house to you, and gave his wives into your embrace. I gave you the house of Israel and Judah. If that was too little, I would have given even more. Why have you despised the LORD's word by doing what is evil in his eyes? You have struck down Uriah the Hittite with the sword and taken his wife as your own. You used the Ammonites to kill him. Because of that, because you despised me and took the wife of Uriah the Hittite as your own, the sword will never leave your own house.

NATHAN: This is what the LORD says: I am making trouble come against you from inside your own family. Before your very eyes I will take your wives away and give them to your friend, and he will have sex with your wives in broad daylight. You did what you did secretly, but I will do what I am doing before all Israel in the light of day.

STORYTELLER #1: David was very sorry and confessed his sin.

NATHAN: The LORD has removed your sin. You won't die. However, because you have utterly disrespected the LORD by doing this, the son born to you will definitely die.

STORYTELLER #2: Then Nathan went home.

Take the next few minutes to read through the questions below and jot down your responses. When you're done, find a partner and discuss the story with them.

Journal Questions

• What does David's response to Nathan's parable reveal about him?

• Why was it so easy for David to excuse his actions until now?

• Is there anyone in your life who is willing to tell you what you need to hear—even when it's unpleasant?

BUILD

Work together with your group to make a children's book that retells today's story. You can keep the story the same, or you can add details and place the story in the present day. You'll have fifteen minutes to outline your book and make the pages. The book needs to be at least four pages long.

Use the space provided on this page and the following page to outline your storybook with your group.

AFTER

Prayer and Support

David could have avoided this terrible situation if he'd had someone to speak truth to him and to remind him to stay focused on serving his people. This week talk to a friend whom you trust about a sin or destructive pattern you struggle with. Ask them to pray for you and to support you in establishing better habits.

Who do you trust that you can talk to this week?

_____

What can they pray for you about?

_____

_____

Our Best Selves

Because he was close to David, Nathan was able to push David to repent and change. Positive words from our friends can be just as powerful as negative messages. This week tell a friend something you admire about them. Encouragement reminds us to be our best selves.

Who can you encourage this week?

_____

AFTER

Truth to Power

This week post something on social media that reminds you of the faithfulness of Nathan in speaking truth to power. Write a short explanation about why it's important for us to always stand up against wrongdoing, even when it means we have to confront friends.

Write down three ideas for something you could post on social media this week that reminds you about the importance of speaking truth to power.

1) _____

2) _____

3) _____

PRAYER

Thank you, God, for people who know us well enough to remind us of who you want us to be. Thank you that our sin is never so big that it has to define us. Help us to be brave enough to be honest with each other. Amen.

A Little More . . .

Q: What happened to Bathsheba after this story?

A: That's an excellent question! We have a tendency to focus too much on David, Uriah, and Nathan, and often Bathsheba can get lost in the shuffle.

Bathsheba would eventually give birth to a son. We're told in 2 Samuel 12:16 that David begged for the child's life, but the child would die after seven days. After the death of their child, Bathsheba would become pregnant again and give birth to Solomon, who would succeed David as king.

When David died, there was some intrigue around who would succeed him on the throne. In 1 Kings 2, we're told that Bathsheba plays an integral role in securing the throne for Solomon over his half-brother, Adonijah.

The last appearance of Bathsheba comes in a rather unexpected place. In Matthew 1:6, Bathsheba is mentioned as part of Jesus' genealogy. However, she is still listed as Uriah's wife. Even generations later, Bathsheba is mainly remembered in relationship to the men who dominated her life.

Solomon Humbly Asks for Wisdom

Summary

This week you will learn about Solomon's request for wisdom from God. You will also discuss the importance of seeing yourself as a servant and understanding your own limitations.

Overview

- **Sync** with the story by imagining what you would wish for if given the chance.
- **Tour** through Solomon's encounter with God by reconstructing the passage as a group.
- **Reveal** what we can learn from Solomon by comparing his story to other stories about leadership and responsibility.
- **Build** on what you've learned by looking at how wisdom impacted the rest of Solomon's life.
- **After** the lesson, choose an activity to help you reflect on your own responsibilities and the need for God's help.

Anchor Point

- 1 Kings 3:7, 9—*And now, LORD my God, you have made me, your servant, king in my father David's place. But I'm young and inexperienced. I know next to nothing. . . . Please give your servant a discerning mind in order to govern your people and to distinguish good from evil, because no one is able to govern this important people of yours without your help.*

SYNC

"Wildest Dreams" Charades

Instructions

1) On the piece of paper you've received, write down what you would ask for if you were given one wish.
2) Without showing anyone, fold it in half and put it in the hat.

Rules

1) Someone will draw one of the wishes from the hat.
2) They will have two minutes to act out whatever is on the paper.
3) They cannot use words or sounds.
4) If they are stuck, they will ring the bell and choose someone from the audience to help them act out what is on the paper.
5) Whoever guesses correctly will choose who goes next.

• What do you think your wish says about you?

When Solomon found himself in a similar situation, he asked God for something unexpected. Today we'll talk about what his request reveals about him.

"Wildest Dreams" Collage

If you had one wish, what would you ask for?

_____

_____

Together with your group, you're going to make a collage that represents all of your collective wishes. You can use any words or images that you associate with your answer. If you're looking for something specific, let everyone else know so they can be on the lookout too. We'll take about ten minutes to make our collage.

• What do you think your wish says about you?

When Solomon found himself in a similar situation, he asked God for something unexpected. Today we'll talk about what his request reveals about him.

Write out the verse or verses you chose.

How did the meaning of the verse(s) you originally chose change when you read it in context?

What does Solomon's answer tell us about Solomon?

We've seen that King Saul and King David each had their own ideas about what it meant to be a king. How do you think Solomon's view of being a king is different?

REVEAL FATH●M

Take the next few minutes to respond to the prompts you see below.

Journal Questions

• Think of three stories from popular books, TV shows, movies, or the news that involve young people and leadership or responsibility. What do these stories—or people's reactions to them—imply about these topics?

• How does the picture of Solomon from today's story compare to all of these messages?

Read through the summaries below with your group, and choose one of the stories to explore more.

Summaries of Events in King Solomon's Reign

1 Kings 3:16-28

• Two women come to Solomon with a custody dispute. Each only has her own word to go on. Solomon creates a way to discover the baby's rightful mother.

1 Kings 4:29–5:18

• Solomon becomes a botanist and zoologist, and news of his wisdom spreads. Nearby kings begin to curry favor with him.

1 Kings 10

• The queen of Sheba visits Solomon to witness his fabled wisdom.

Once you've chosen, read through the passage and then work with your group to rework the story into a one-minute skit about what would have happened if Solomon hadn't asked for wisdom. Then you'll do a one-minute skit showing how things actually played out in the Bible.

1 Kings 3:16-28

Sometime later, two prostitutes came and stood before the king. One of them said, "Please, Your Majesty, listen: This woman and I have been living in the same house. I gave birth while she was there. This woman gave birth three days after I did. We stayed together. Apart from the two of us, there was no one else in the house. This woman's son died one night when she rolled over him. She got up in the middle of the night and took my son from my side while I was asleep. She laid him on her chest and laid her dead son on mine. When I got up in the morning to nurse my son, he was dead! But when I looked more closely in the daylight, it turned out that it wasn't my son—not the baby I had birthed."

The other woman said, "No! My son is alive! Your son is the dead one."

But the first woman objected, "No! Your son is dead! My son is alive!" In this way they argued back and forth in front of the king.

The king said, "This one says, 'My son is alive and your son is dead.' The other one says, 'No! Your son is dead and my son is alive.' Get me a sword!" They brought a sword to the king. Then the king said, "Cut the living child in two! Give half to one woman and half to the other woman."

Then the woman whose son was still alive said to the king, "Please, Your Majesty, give her the living child; please don't kill him," for she had great love for her son.

But the other woman said, "If I can't have him, neither will you. Cut the child in half."

Then the king answered, "Give the first woman the living newborn. Don't kill him. She is his mother."

All Israel heard about the judgment that the king made. Their respect for the king grew because they saw that God's wisdom was in him so he could execute justice.

Use the space provided to work out your two skits.

1 Kings 4:29–5:18

And God gave Solomon wisdom and very great understanding—insight as long as the seashore itself. Solomon's wisdom was greater than all the famous Easterners, greater even than all the wisdom of Egypt. He was wiser than anyone, more wise than Ethan the Ezrahite or Mahol's sons: Heman, Calcol, and Darda. His reputation was known throughout the region. Solomon spoke three thousand proverbs and one thousand five songs. He described the botany of trees, whether the cedar in Lebanon or the hyssop that grows out of the wall. He also described cattle, birds, anything that crawls on the ground, and fish. People came from everywhere to listen to Solomon's wisdom; even the earth's kings who had heard about his wisdom came!

Because King Hiram of Tyre was loyal to David throughout his rule, Hiram sent his servants to Solomon when he heard that Solomon had become king after his father. Solomon sent the following message to Hiram: "You know that my father David wasn't able to build a temple for the name of the LORD my God. This was because of the enemies that fought him on all sides until the LORD put them under the soles of his feet. Now the LORD my God has given me peace on every side, without enemies or misfortune. So I'm planning to build a temple for the name of the LORD my God, just as the LORD indicated to my father David, 'I will give you a son to follow you on your throne. He will build the temple for my name.' Now give the order and have the cedars of Lebanon cut down for me. My servants will work with your servants. I'll pay your servants whatever price you set, because you know we have no one here who is skilled in cutting wood like the Sidonians."

Hiram was thrilled when he heard Solomon's message. He said, "Today the LORD is blessed because he has given David a wise son who is in charge of this great people." Hiram sent word back to Solomon: "I have heard your message to me. I will do as you wish with the cedar and pinewood. My servants will bring the wood down the Lebanon Mountains to the sea. I'll make rafts out of them and float them on the sea to the place you specify. There I'll dismantle them, and you can carry them away. Now, as for what you must do for me in return, I ask you to provide for my royal house."

1 Kings 4:29–5:18 (cont.)

So Hiram gave Solomon all the cedar and pinewood that he wanted. In return, Solomon gave an annual gift to Hiram of twenty thousand kors of wheat to eat, and twenty thousand kors of pure oil for his palace use. Now the LORD made Solomon wise, just as he had promised. Solomon and Hiram made a covenant and had peace.

King Solomon called up a work gang of thirty thousand workers from all over Israel. He sent ten thousand to work in Lebanon each month. Then they would spend two months at home. Adoniram was in charge of the work gang. Solomon had 70,000 laborers and 80,000 stonecutters in the highlands. This doesn't include Solomon's 3,300 supervisors in charge of the work, who had oversight over the laborers. At the king's command, they quarried huge stones of the finest quality in order to lay the temple's foundation with carefully cut stone. The craftsmen of Solomon and Hiram, along with those of Byblos, prepared the timber and the stones for the construction of the temple.

Use the space provided to work out your two skits.

1 Kings 10:1-13

When the queen of Sheba heard reports about Solomon, due to the LORD's name, she came to test him with riddles. Accompanying her to Jerusalem was a huge entourage with camels carrying spices, a large amount of gold, and precious stones. After she arrived, she told Solomon everything that was on her mind. Solomon answered all her questions; nothing was too difficult for him to answer. When the queen of Sheba saw how wise Solomon was, the palace he had built, the food on his table, the servants' quarters, the function and dress of his attendants, his cupbearers, and the entirely burned offerings that he offered at the LORD's temple, it took her breath away.

"The report I heard about your deeds and wisdom when I was still at home is true," she said to the king. "I didn't believe it until I came and saw it with my own eyes. In fact, the half of it wasn't even told to me! You have far more wisdom and wealth than I was told. Your people and these servants who continually serve you and get to listen to your wisdom are truly happy! Bless the LORD your God because he was pleased to place you on Israel's throne. Because the LORD loved Israel with an eternal love, the LORD made you king to uphold justice and righteousness."

The queen gave the king one hundred twenty kikkars of gold, a great quantity of spice, and precious stones. Never again has so much spice come to Israel as when the queen of Sheba gave this gift to King Solomon. Hiram's fleet went to Ophir and brought back gold, much almug wood, and precious stones. The king used the almug wood to make parapets for the LORD's temple and for the royal palace as well as lyres and harps for the musicians. To this day, that much almug wood hasn't come into or been seen in Israel. King Solomon gave the queen of Sheba everything she wanted and all that she had asked for, in addition to what he had already given her from his own personal funds. Then she and her servants returned to her homeland.

Use the space provided to work out your two skits.

AFTER

What Would You Ask for?

Solomon asked God for wisdom, knowing that God would provide the gift. Partner with a friend and share what spiritual gift you each feel you need from God. Pray for each other throughout the week. In a few days, send an encouraging text to your partner to remind them that you are praying with them.

Remember the Help You've Received

We've all had people who have helped us out in the past. Sometimes we ask for that help, and sometimes they do it without us having to say anything. This week thank someone via email or social media who has helped you achieve something you couldn't have done on your own.

Over Your Head

From his request, we learn that Solomon knew he was in over his head as king. That happens to all of us from time to time, and it's something we learn from. This week ask a parent or mentor about a time when they felt overwhelmed and what they did in response.

PRAYER FATH●M

Recite the following prayer together.

Dear God, thank you for the stories we have heard over the past few weeks. Please inspire us to be humble and to give you glory in all that we do. Amen.

Takeaway

In only four weeks, we've visited two kings—David and Solomon—on the best days of their lives, and witnessed two—Saul and David—at their worst. Each king struggles in his own way to lead the people and conduct himself well, but a common thread connects them when they are at their best: humility.

Humility is a tricky word to define. Some people connect it with *humiliation,* but while the words are related, the connection isn't quite right. In general, humility means thinking about yourself as no better and no worse than other people. Think of it this way: if you believe you are the worst person in the world, you've actually assigned yourself a pretty special position! Being humble means we turn our attention toward other people. We recognize when we are not the smartest, best-looking, holiest, fastest, or friendliest person in the room, but we aren't afraid, either, to offer the gifts and talents we do have in service of others. When we hide, disparage, and undervalue ourselves, we're often acting defensively against the risk of really putting ourselves out there. A humble person, on the other hand, knows that their worth isn't determined by others' opinions, and doesn't have to be guarded as a result. Do you know anyone with a quiet, refreshing self-confidence like that?

At his best, David is an excellent example. When he dances before God in a parade, he's showing that he doesn't have anything to prove. As the saying goes, "Humility is not thinking less of yourself; it's thinking of yourself less." David is so focused on worshipping God and celebrating with his people that he doesn't care how he looks.

At the other extreme, Saul is never confident enough to forget himself. He was once reluctant to become king, and always seems to act out of insecurity—often leading him to make poor choices. When he is commanded to kill the king of the Amalekites, he decides he has a better idea to turn the situation to his own advantage. He tries to curry favor with his men and impress everyone else by parading the king and the livestock around as a victory party, but in the end, he only looks like a fool in a public confrontation with Samuel, who forcefully reminds him that being king doesn't entitle Saul to do whatever he wants.

David, too, falls into the trap of entitlement. He thinks he can have Bathsheba without any consequences, and spins a web of sin and deceit. Maybe he even believes that he's gotten away with it, but Bathsheba and Uriah are not the only witnesses. God has seen David's actions too. God punishes David and reminds him that he should have been content with his own wives rather than pridefully and selfishly taking someone else's.

Finally, Solomon shows us what it looks like to be honest about your own capabilities. In contrast to Saul, he doesn't try to hide his weaknesses, but asks God for help. And in contrast to David, he doesn't consider himself entitled to fame and fortune, but considers the people he's responsible for when he makes his request. God sees that Solomon would put fame and fortune to good use, and grants these along with his request for wisdom.

David and Solomon knew, deep down, that they were valuable—and that other people are too. Sometimes that knowledge leads us, like David, to be so self-forgetful that we don't care what others think of us. Other times, humility helps us to be introspective enough to recognize our specific strengths and limitations in serving God, like Solomon. Whatever the circumstance, humble people are secure enough in their own identities to find joy in others rather than constantly competing for validation, a feeling most of us can remember from the best days of our lives.

Explore More

1 Samuel 18:1-5

As soon as David had finished talking with Saul, Jonathan's life became bound up with David's life, and Jonathan loved David as much as himself. From that point forward, Saul kept David in his service and wouldn't allow him to return to his father's household. And Jonathan and David made a covenant together because Jonathan loved David as much as himself. Jonathan took off the robe he was wearing and gave it to David, along with his armor, as well as his sword, his bow, and his belt. David went out and was successful in every mission Saul sent him to do. So Saul placed him in charge of the soldiers, and this pleased all the troops as well as Saul's servants

Application

• The Bible is not shy about describing David and Jonathan's friendship in very strong terms. Jonathan's friendship is an important part of David's life, and ultimately saves David's life. Having such a strong bond with another man is another way in which David doesn't fit the stereotypical mold of a macho warrior.

Questions

1. How do you encourage and care for your friends?
2. Is it a sign of strength to go it alone?
3. Do you think friendship should be a priority, like faith and family?

2 Samuel 7:4-7, 11-13

But that very night the LORD's word came to Nathan: Go to my servant David and tell him: This is what the LORD says: You are not the one to build the temple for me to live in. In fact, I haven't lived in a temple from the day I brought Israel out of Egypt until now. Instead, I have been traveling around in a tent and in a dwelling. Throughout my traveling around with the Israelites, did I ever ask any of Israel's tribal leaders I appointed to shepherd my people: Why haven't you built me a cedar temple? (4-7)

And the LORD declares to you that the LORD will make a dynasty for you. When the time comes for you to die and you lie down with your ancestors, I will raise up your descendant—one of your very own children—to succeed you, and I will establish his kingdom. He will build a temple for my name, and I will establish his royal throne forever. (11-13)

Application

- David has declared his intention to build a temple for God, but God makes it clear that God is in no need of a house. God says that God will "establish a house" for David instead. David's good intentions were misguided. He was so focused on doing something for God that he forgot God didn't need his assistance.

Questions

1. Have you ever gotten so caught up in doing something for God that you missed out on noticing God's blessings?
2. Where has God "dwelt in a tent" in accompanying you on your journey?

CPSIA information can be obtained
at www.ICGtesting.com
Printed in the USA
LVHW01s0424220218
567325LV00011B/250/P

9 781501 841583